Laughs and Giggles: Funny Teacher Appreciation Jokes for Kids

Clip art and fonts were created by:

https://edu-clips.com/

http://www.teacherspayteachers.com/Store/Hello-Literacy

First Edition: April 2019

www.TeacherNyla.com

This book belongs to:

_____

Table of Contents

Teacher

Funny
Jokes

Giggle these riddles!

6

Q: Why did the teacher wear sunglasses to school?

Q: Why did the teacher say that a triangle is adorable?

A: Because her students were bright!

A: Because it has acute angles.

Q: Why didn't the teacher want to close her eyes during the school day?

Q: Why did the teacher marry the janitor?

A: There would be no pupils to see!

A: Because he swept her off her feet!

Q: Why did the teacher jump into the pond?

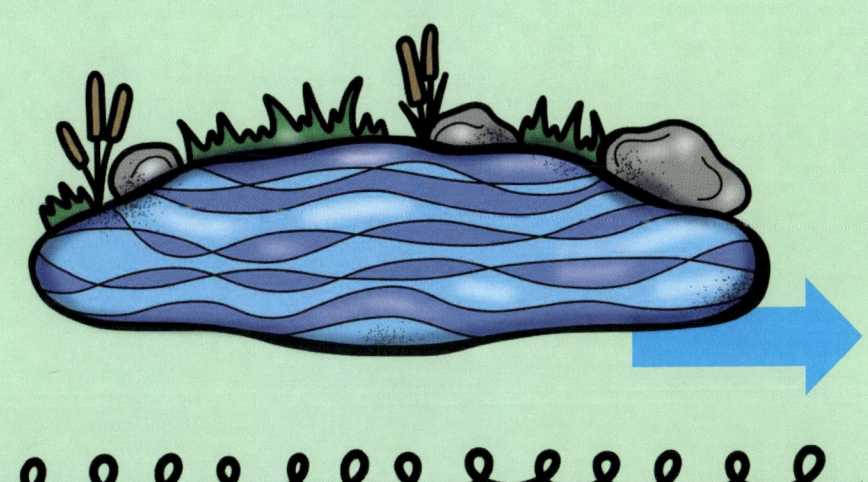

Q: Why did the music teacher need a ladder?

A: To test the waters!

A: To reach the higher notes!

Q: What kind of meals do math teachers eat?

Q: What happened when the teacher tied all the kids' shoe laces together?

A: Square meals!

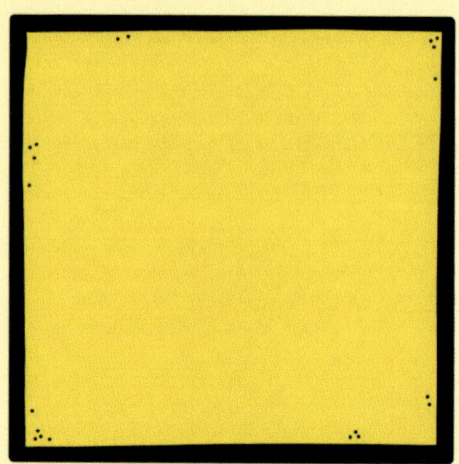

A: They had a class trip!

Q: What's the difference between a teacher and a steam train?

Q: Why did the teacher write the lesson on the windows?

A: The first says "Spit out that bubble gum" and the second says "chew chew" (choo-choo).

A: He wanted the lesson to be very clear.

Q: Which dessert does a math teacher like the most?

Q: Why was the voice teacher so good at baseball?

A: Pi!

A: Because he had the perfect pitch!

Q: Why did the Cyclops teacher have such an easy day of school?

Q: Which season does a math teacher like the most?

A: He only had one pupil!

A: Sum-mer!

Q: What do you get when you cross a teacher with a calculator?

Q: Where do teachers with a sweet tooth like to teach?

A: Someone you can always count on.

A: In sundae school!

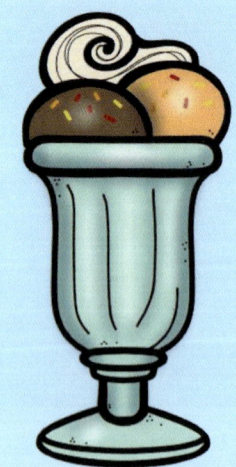

Q: Why did the math teacher hand out eye glasses during class?

Q: Who is the most famous Physical Education teacher?

A: To help his students with their di-vison.

A: Jim Nasium.

Q: What do math teachers eat on Thanksgiving?

Q: Why did the teacher bring her slippers to school for Teachers Appreciation Week?

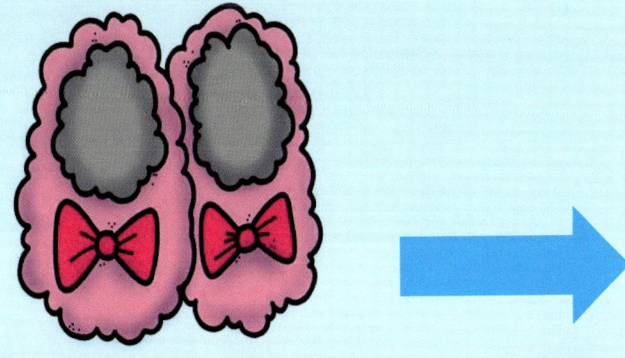

A: Pumpkin Pi!

A: To wear them in the teachers'

lounge!

Teacher

Knock-knock Jokes

Knock, knock!

Who's there?

To.

To who?

Knock, knock!

Who's there?

Four eggs.

Four eggs who?

It's to whom.

Four eggsample...

Knock, knock!

Who's there?

Rita.

Rita who?

Knock, knock!

Who's there?

Carson.

Carson who?

Rita little more and find out!

Carson in school is not allowed!

Knock, knock!

Who's there?

Annetta.

Annetta who?

Knock, knock!

Who's there?

M. Cindy.

M. Cindy who?

Annetta wise crack and you're outta here!

M. Cindy you to the principal's office.

Teacher

Tongue Twisters

How fast can you say them?

Did Miss notice the notice?

A synonym for cinnamon is a cinnamon synonym.

Don't trouble trouble till trouble troubles you.

Mix, Miss Mix!

Three teachers thinking thoughtful thoughts.

These thousand tricky tongue twisters trip thrillingly off the tongue.

Bonus Joke

Q: Who is your best friend at school?

A: Your princi-PAL.

Thank you for reading this book!

Have you read these other titles in this series?

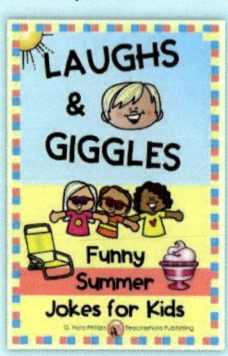

www.TeacherNyla.com